UNDERSTANDING AMERICAN DEMOCRACY

FAIR ELECTIONS AND VOTING RIGHTS

by Sheryl Normandeau

BrightPoint Press

San Diego, CA

© 2024 BrightPoint Press
an imprint of ReferencePoint Press, Inc.
Printed in the United States

For more information, contact:
BrightPoint Press
PO Box 27779
San Diego, CA 92198
www.BrightPointPress.com

ALL RIGHTS RESERVED.

No part of this work covered by the copyright hereon may be reproduced or used in any form or by any means—graphic, electronic, or mechanical, including photocopying, recording, taping, web distribution, or information storage retrieval systems—without the written permission of the publisher.

LIBRARY OF CONGRESS CATALOGING-IN-PUBLICATION DATA

Names: Normandeau, Sheryl, author.
Title: Fair elections and voting rights / By Sheryl Normandeau.
Description: San Diego, CA: BrightPoint, [2024] | Series: Understanding American democracy | Includes bibliographical references and index. | Audience: Ages 13 | Audience: Grades 7-9
Identifiers: LCCN 2023015136 (print) | LCCN 2023015137 (eBook) | ISBN 9781678206925 (hardcover) | ISBN 9781678206932 (eBook)
Subjects: LCSH: Voting--United States--Juvenile literature. | Elections--United States--Juvenile literature. | Suffrage--United States--Juvenile literature. | Democracy--United States--Juvenile literature.
Classification: LCC JF1001 .N65 2024 (print) | LCC JF1001 (eBook) | DDC 324.6/20973--dc23/eng/20230403
LC record available at https://lccn.loc.gov/2023015136
LC eBook record available at https://lccn.loc.gov/2023015137

CONTENTS

AT A GLANCE	**4**
INTRODUCTION MAKING YOUR MARK	**6**
CHAPTER ONE WHY DO WE VOTE?	**12**
CHAPTER TWO TYPES OF ELECTIONS	**22**
CHAPTER THREE THE HISTORY OF US ELECTIONS	**36**
CHAPTER FOUR ELECTION CONCERNS AND DEBATES	**48**
Glossary	58
Source Notes	59
For Further Research	60
Index	62
Image Credits	63
About the Author	64

AT A GLANCE

- The Constitution is a document that explains the structures and processes of the US government. It outlines the rights and responsibilities of US citizens.

- The United States is a democracy. In a democracy, citizens vote for government leaders in elections. These leaders represent the citizens.

- In a fair election, everyone has the opportunity to vote. All votes are counted. People cannot be prevented from voting or told whom to vote for. Everyone must have equal access to polling places.

- There are many types of elections, including primaries, midterms, and local elections. The procedures for each type of election differ. Individual states may run elections in different ways.

- The US president is elected every four years. Through primaries and caucuses, each political party selects one nominee to appear on the presidential ballot.

- Voting rights have changed over time. African Americans, Native Americans, and women have had to fight for the right to vote. Throughout history, amendments have been added to the Constitution to protect these citizens' voting rights.

- Some voters worry about election fraud, foreign interference, and mail-in ballots. They wonder if elections are secure and fair.

- Some people disagree about voting practices such as voter IDs. Several states require voters to show photo IDs at polling places. Some people say this is unfair and could prevent people from voting.

INTRODUCTION

MAKING YOUR MARK

Rashad is eighteen years old. Today, he is voting for the first time. This year is a presidential election. Voters will decide who the next US president will be.

Rashad came to his **polling place** prepared. Before Election Day, he registered to vote. Rashad also researched the

candidates for other races in his state. He looked at each candidate's website. He read about their views on current issues. Candidates from one **political party** share Rashad's views. They promise actions that

Many polling places use paper ballots for voting. To vote for a candidate, a voter must fill in the oval next to the candidate's name.

Some polling places use ballot counting machines. Voters put their completed paper ballots into the machine, which scans the marks on the ballots.

he thinks will help the country. Now Rashad knows whom he wants to vote for. It's time to put his mark on the ballot.

A poll worker hands Rashad a ballot. She directs him to a voting booth. Here, Rashad can mark his ballot privately.

The ballot looks a lot like a multiple-choice test. To vote for a candidate, Rashad must fill in the oval next to the candidate's name. He carefully fills out his ballot. Then a poll worker helps Rashad put the ballot into a voting machine. This counts his votes.

The worker smiles. She hands Rashad an "I Voted" sticker. He proudly puts the sticker on his shirt. By casting his vote, Rashad knows he's making his voice heard.

PARTICIPATING IN ELECTIONS

The United States is a democracy. This means US **citizens** shape how the

By voting in elections, US citizens have a say in how the government is run.

government is run. They choose leaders

to represent them. They do this by voting

in elections. Elections are supposed to be fair. But sometimes voting is done unfairly. It might not include everyone. Or some people might make it hard for others to vote. This can make people mistrust the voting process. Others may not want to vote. They may think their voices don't matter. This can disrupt democracy.

The first US presidential election was in 1789. Elections have changed since then. Throughout history, people have worked to make elections fair. People continue to make sure everyone has a say in the government.

1

WHY DO WE VOTE?

The country's founders created a democratic system of government. They wanted US citizens to play a role in the government. This way, citizens would have a say in government decisions. They would be able to choose their leaders.

THE US CONSTITUTION

By the mid-1700s, there were thirteen colonies in North America. They were ruled by England. England made laws

In 1787, state leaders met in Philadelphia, Pennsylvania, to create the US Constitution. This meeting was called the Constitutional Convention.

for the colonists to follow. Many colonists thought England treated them unjustly. They wanted to govern themselves. This led to the Revolutionary War (1775–1783). The colonists fought for independence. They won the war and formed a new nation.

The colonies became the first US states. Each state had its own government. But the national government had little power.

REPRESENTING THE PEOPLE

In a democracy, a country's people run the government. In the United States, elected officials are representatives of the people. This means they serve them. They make decisions based on what the people want. Elected officials must listen to the people. They must respect their wishes.

It couldn't raise an army or set taxes. A stronger central government was needed.

In 1787, state leaders met in Philadelphia. They wrote the Constitution. This document outlined how the government would work. It gave citizens the power to elect leaders. It also split the government into three branches.

The legislative branch is Congress. It creates laws. The judicial branch is the courts. It interprets the laws. The executive branch is led by the president. It ensures laws are followed.

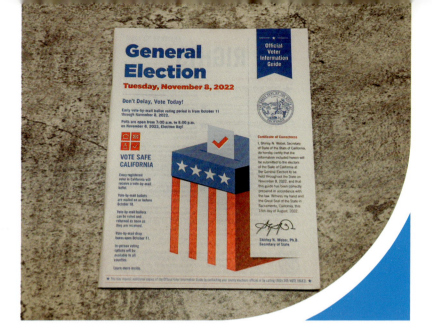

To make informed decisions, it is important for voters to research candidates in an election. Some states, such as California, provide voter guides.

WHY IS VOTING IMPORTANT?

Voting ensures that democracy happens. When people vote, they show the government which issues they care about. Kristen Dahlgren is a journalist. She thinks everyone should vote. "When you vote you choose someone who can represent you and your interests in the government," she said. "You can also vote on issues that are important to you. So if you want your roads to be fixed or a new school to be built, you can vote for these things."[1]

Government leaders make decisions about issues such as taxes. Voters decide who will make these decisions. They can elect leaders who share their views.

WHAT MAKES ELECTIONS FAIR?

In a fair US election, all citizens have the chance to vote. People can vote for the candidates they want. No one can tell

Poll workers and election officials make sure ballots are counted accurately. They are also responsible for processing mail-in ballots.

a person how to vote. Each vote is also equally powerful.

In a fair election, all ballots must be counted accurately. Poll workers work hard to avoid mistakes. Ballots cannot be missed or counted twice. Election results must be announced correctly. All candidates must respect the results too, even if they lose. In a fair election, citizens must receive reliable information about candidates. Candidates must also meet requirements for the position they are seeking.

Citizens must have fair access to polling places too. Polls open and close at specific times. Some voters may be unable to get to polling places before closing time. Others live far away. These people need another way to vote. Some states offer early voting or absentee voting. These allow people to vote early. They can vote in person or by mail. Voters fill out mail-in ballots at home.

Polling places must also be accessible. Not all voters speak English. They may be unable to understand election information. To help, polling places hire workers who speak different languages. They also provide translated voter forms. Polling places must help voters with disabilities too. They must have accessible entrances, such as wheelchair ramps.

Sometimes people try to prevent others from voting. This is called voter suppression.

Polling places must have accessible entrances for voters with disabilities. They must also provide translated materials for non-English speakers.

People may do this to affect election results.

They make it hard for some people to vote.

Some states require voters to show a photo identification card, or ID. Some people think this prevents unfair voting. But others say it suppresses voters. Some people cannot afford to buy an ID.

2

TYPES OF ELECTIONS

There are many types of elections. Some are large. Others are small. Governments at all levels hold elections. Local governments run towns and cities. In local elections, people vote for roles such as mayor. These leaders are elected by people living in their regions. In state elections, people vote for positions in their state's government. This includes roles such as governor. In federal elections, people vote for national positions. This includes the president.

Presidential candidates often speak at rallies and events throughout the country to gain support.

PRESIDENTIAL AND CONGRESSIONAL ELECTIONS

Presidential elections happen every four years. A candidate must follow several steps to become president. First, the candidate announces that he or she is running for president. Then he or she must be selected as a nominee. The candidate must be chosen by his or her political party. This is done through caucuses and primaries.

Caucuses are meetings held by political parties. Only party members can attend closed caucuses. But the public can attend open caucuses. During caucuses, party members split into groups based on which candidate they support. Each group tries to get supporters. These supporters vote to choose **delegates** for the candidate. Whoever gets the most delegates wins the nomination. Later, the delegates will represent the candidate at national party conventions.

QUALIFICATIONS FOR PRESIDENT

To run for president, a person must be at least thirty-five years old. He or she must have been born a US citizen. He or she must also have lived in the country for at least fourteen years. When a candidate has over $5,000 for his or her **campaign**, he or she must register with the Federal Election Commission. This group enforces rules about campaign funds.

During caucuses, party members discuss who they think the best presidential candidate will be. They split into groups based on whom they support.

State primaries are another way to choose delegates. These are held by state governments. During primaries, people vote for candidates they want to see on the ballot. This decides how many delegates each candidate gets.

Once delegates are selected, each political party holds a national convention. Here, delegates vote for presidential candidates. They must support the same candidates they supported in the primary or caucus. Whoever wins becomes the party's presidential nominee.

Congressional elections happen every two years. Voters elect members of the House of Representatives and Senate. Representatives serve two-year terms. They run for election every two years. Each one represents a state district. They are elected by voters in that district. Senators have six-year terms. Every two years, one-third of senators run for election. Congressional candidates must be nominated.

Some congressional elections are midterms. These happen halfway between presidential elections. Voters elect House representatives and some senators.

During some elections, states may ask voters to decide on ballot measures. These appear on voters' ballots. They may be proposed laws or questions about current issues.

Before elections, voters often receive flyers and political ads in the mail. These may include arguments about certain ballot measures.

During midterms, the president cannot lose his or her job. But how people vote during midterms is important. It shows how happy they are with the government. Sometimes midterms affect the president's party. It may lose seats in Congress.

29

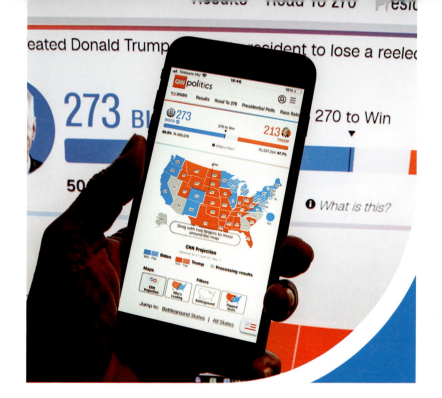

During a presidential election, many news outlets publish live reports. People can use their phones to keep track of who wins electoral votes.

THE ELECTORAL COLLEGE

On Election Day, people cast votes for president. These are called popular votes. But voters do not vote directly for president. The electoral college does. This is a process used to elect the president.

Richard H. Pildes is a professor. He says, "When you go to vote, you are actually voting for representatives in the electoral college in your state who will then vote for the president."[2] These representatives are electors. When a candidate wins a state's popular vote, electors from his or her party are chosen to participate in the electoral college vote. After Election Day, 538 electors cast electoral votes to elect the president. To win, 270 votes are needed.

Most states have a winner-takes-all system. Whoever wins the popular vote gets all the state's electors. But Maine and

Nebraska split electoral votes. Whoever wins the state-wide vote gets two electoral votes. But state districts can each award one electoral vote to the popular vote winner in their district.

The electoral college gives states with smaller populations a fair say in elections.

FAITHLESS ELECTORS

Electors are supposed to vote for their party's chosen candidate. But sometimes electors vote differently. These are called faithless electors. Since 1789, there have been more than 150 faithless electors. Some states have laws that prevent electors from voting against the people's will. Faithless electors can lose their vote or be fined.

Every state gets a certain number of electors. This is based on its population. In 2020, Vermont's population was 643,007. It had three electoral votes. California's population was over 39 million. It had fifty-five votes. A state's number of electoral votes is equal to its number of Congress members. Every state has two senators. But its number of representatives depends on its population.

The electoral vote usually matches the popular vote. But sometimes it doesn't. In 2016, Donald Trump lost the popular vote by 3 million votes. But he still won the presidency. This made people wonder if the electoral college should still be used. But it is in the Constitution. Getting rid of it would require passing an amendment.

VOTING SYSTEMS

Some states use different voting systems. Votes can be counted differently. One method is first-past-the-post. The candidate with the most votes wins.

Other places use two-round systems. These involve voting rounds. The first round decides the top two candidates. In the second round, voters choose between the

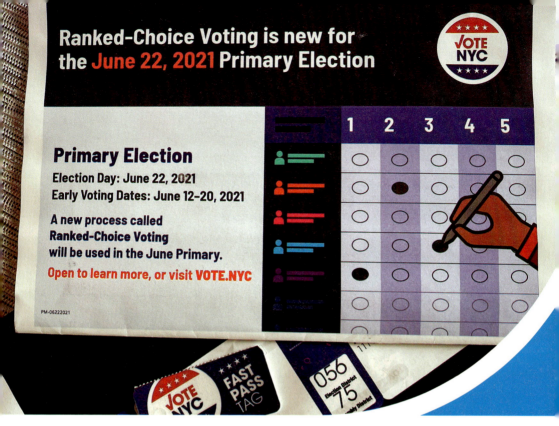

Many places in the United States are embracing ranked-choice voting. Some people believe it better represents voters' viewpoints.

top two. In instant-runoff voting, voters rank candidates. A voter's top candidate may not get enough votes. If this happens, her next-ranked candidate gets her vote. This method is often called ranked-choice voting.

3

THE HISTORY OF US ELECTIONS

US elections have changed over time. The country's founders left voting rules up to each state. But many states limited who could vote. In most states, only white men who owned property could vote. Many people did not have a say in the government.

BLACK AMERICAN VOTING RIGHTS

When the Constitution was written, Black people were not considered citizens. By the 1700s, slavery was a common practice. Black people were kidnapped from Africa.

The Fifteenth Amendment was added to the Constitution in 1870. It gave Black men the right to vote.

They were enslaved in the United States. In southern states, farmers forced enslaved people to harvest crops. But in northern states, many people thought slavery was wrong. Tensions rose between northern and southern states. This led to the American Civil War (1861–1865).

The North won the war. Amendments, or changes, were added to the Constitution. The Thirteenth Amendment ended slavery. In 1868, the Fourteenth Amendment gave citizenship to Black Americans. In 1870, the Fifteenth Amendment said people could not be denied the right to vote based on race.

Throughout the 1960s, many people fought to win voting rights for Black Americans. They participated in protests and marches.

But in some southern states, Black Americans were still prevented from voting. They faced threats at the polls. Some states set poll taxes. These required voters to pay a fee. Many Black people had been formerly enslaved. They could not afford these taxes. Some states also required voters to pass reading tests. Many Black Americans had not been able to go to school. Many couldn't pass the tests. Other states had grandfather clauses. These said people could vote if their grandfathers had voted. This allowed poor white people to vote without paying poll taxes. But most Black Americans' grandfathers had never had voting rights.

Over the next decades, Black Americans fought for equal voting rights. During the 1960s, many people took part in the Civil Rights Movement. They led protests and marches. In 1965, the Voting Rights Act

Women who fought for the vote were called suffragists. They organized large parades, marches, and demonstrations.

passed. It banned poll taxes and other unfair voting practices.

WOMEN'S VOTING RIGHTS

The Constitution did not give women voting rights. By 1868, only men were allowed to vote. Women were still excluded.

In the late 1800s and early 1900s, many women fought for **suffrage**. In 1869, suffragists formed the American Woman Suffrage Association (AWSA). It focused on state and local elections. By 1890, it had won women's voting rights in several states.

In 1869, Susan B. Anthony and Elizabeth Cady Stanton formed the National Woman

THE NATIONAL WOMAN'S PARTY

The National Woman's Party (NWP) formed in 1916. It was led by former NAWSA members. They used aggressive methods to fight for the vote. They led marches and parades. In 1917, they protested outside the White House. Many women were arrested for participating.

Suffrage Association (NWSA). It fought for national voting rights. Anthony said, "There never will be complete equality until women themselves help to make laws and elect lawmakers."[3] In 1890, AWSA and NWSA merged. They formed the National American Woman Suffrage Association (NAWSA). They led marches and protests. In 1920, the Nineteenth Amendment passed. It gave women the right to vote.

NATIVE AMERICAN VOTING RIGHTS

Colonists were not the first people in North America. Before the United States was a country, many Native American nations had their own governments. The Iroquois nation was a democracy of six tribes. It had a central government led by a woman. She chose tribal leaders. The Iroquois held debates and discussions to make laws.

Under the Fifteenth Amendment, Native Americans should have received voting rights. But government officials said the amendment did not include Native Americans. They said that Native Americans needed to be introduced into white culture before they got voting rights. In 1887, the Dawes Act passed. It aimed

President Calvin Coolidge (center) signed the 1924 Snyder Act into law. It gave Native Americans full US citizenship.

to **assimilate** Native Americans into white American culture.

In 1924, the Snyder Act passed. This gave Native Americans full US citizenship. But many states still kept them from voting. Some used poll taxes and reading tests. It took several decades for Native Americans to gain voting rights in every state.

VOTING REQUIREMENTS TODAY

As of 2023, most citizens over eighteen can vote. In all states except North Dakota, voters must register. In twenty-seven states, they need to register before Election Day. Twenty-two states have same-day registration. So does Washington, DC. All states offer mail-in ballots.

Citizens over eighteen can sometimes lose their voting rights. Many states take voting rights away from felons. These are people who have committed serious crimes. Some felons get their voting rights back. But others do not. States may also

In some states, voters are required to show a photo ID such as a driver's license or passport.

take voting rights away from people who they decide are mentally unfit.

Many laws protect voting rights. Some help elderly voters or voters with disabilities. Other laws protect against voter suppression and **fraud**. People continue to protect voting rights.

4
ELECTION CONCERNS AND DEBATES

Modern US elections are more inclusive than they once were. But there are still concerns about unfair elections. Some people worry that votes are not counted accurately. They wonder if ballots are secure. Some voters worry about other countries altering election results. There may also be changes to how votes are counted. Some polling places use voting machines. Others hand-count ballots. This can make people uneasy.

Government officials work to make voting fair and secure. They create secure

Voters have several options for returning mail-in ballots. They can mail them, turn them in at election offices, or drop them in drop boxes.

Some people think mail-in ballots are a good option for elderly voters, sick voters, or voters who cannot make it to polling places in person.

systems. They work to prevent fraud. Poll workers are trained in state election laws. They promise to follow all rules. Other rules say there must always be two or more officials at polling places. This keeps people from tampering with ballots.

MAIL-IN BALLOTS

Voters who cannot vote in person can request mail-in ballots. Some people think these ballots can be used for fraud. They worry about people filling out multiple mail-in ballots.

In 2020, President Donald Trump ran for reelection. He worried about mail-in ballot fraud. Joe Biden won the election. Trump and his supporters claimed the election was stolen. They said there had been mail-in ballot fraud.

But mail-in ballots are designed to be secure. The ballots have two envelopes.

The inner envelope holds the ballot. It is sealed. It is kept secret until counted. Devin James Stone is a lawyer. He says, "A ballot cannot be mailed to a person unless they are an eligible and registered voter. This means that a person must fill out a registration form and have their address

SOCIAL MEDIA AND THE VOTE

Barack Obama ran for president in 2008. He used social media to reach out to voters. By 2016, many candidates used social media. But some people use social media to spread false information. This makes voters believe untrue things. Some social media sites keep track of politicians' accounts. They shut down false information.

confirmed."[4] The voter signs the outer envelope to prove she is a registered voter.

ELECTION INTERFERENCE

During the 2016 US election, people discovered that Russia was trying to sway voting results. It was using social media to influence people. It wanted to affect the way they voted.

Investigators found that Russia did not change the results. But many voters were upset about what happened. It was worrisome that other countries could meddle with US elections.

In some states, there are areas that use electronic voting machines. Voters use these devices to mark their ballots electronically.

Election interference takes many forms. Sometimes people use social media to affect how voters think and act. This can make voters mistrust the electoral process.

54

VOTING MACHINES

Some people worry about how votes are counted. This was an issue during the 2016 presidential election. Russian computer hackers got into US voter registration databases. These contained voter information, such as addresses. This did not change the election results. But it scared many people.

Paper ballots are more secure than electronic ones. Most states use paper ballots. But some states still use electronic voting machines. In the 2020 election, Trump and his supporters complained about these machines. They said the machines were rigged to vote against Trump. In places where results were in question, ballots were recounted. No evidence of voter fraud was found.

US elections continue to change. New issues arise in each election. People disagree about what elections should look like. They worry about unfair voting practices. But people work hard to make elections fair for all citizens. They defend every citizen's right to vote. Voters make a difference too. By voting, they help shape the country's future.

ABSENTEE AND EARLY VOTING IN PRESIDENTIAL ELECTIONS, 2000–2020

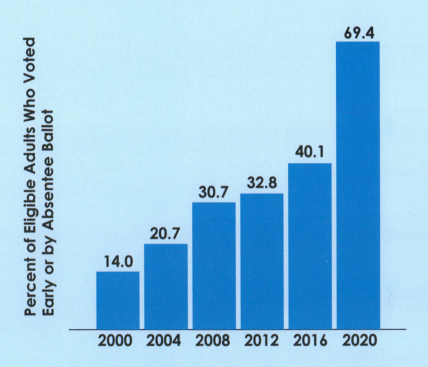

Source: Zachary Scherer, "Majority of Voters Used Nontraditional Methods to Cast Ballots in 2020," United States Census Bureau, *April 29, 2021. www.census.gov.*

In the 2020 presidential election, most Americans chose to vote early or by absentee ballot. One reason for this may have been the COVID-19 pandemic.

GLOSSARY

assimilate
to conform or absorb

campaign
a political plan or strategy to achieve a goal

candidates
people who want to be considered for a government office

citizens
people legally recognized as being part of a country

delegates
people serving as representatives at a government meeting

fraud
dishonest or unfair actions used to achieve a certain goal

political party
an organized group of people who share similar political ideas

polling place
a location where people go to vote

suffrage
the right to vote

SOURCE NOTES

CHAPTER ONE: WHY DO WE VOTE?

1. Quoted in "The Importance of Voting," *YouTube*, May 5, 2020. www.youtube.com.

CHAPTER TWO: TYPES OF ELECTIONS

2. Quoted in Madison Mills, "The Electoral College Explained," *New York Times*, November 9, 2016. www.nytimes.com.

CHAPTER THREE: THE HISTORY OF US ELECTIONS

3. Quoted in "Documented Rights: Section III," *National Archives*, n.d. www.archives.gov.

CHAPTER FOUR: ELECTION CONCERNS AND DEBATES

4. Devin James Stone, "The Truth About Voting by Mail and Election Fraud: LegalEagle's Real Law Review," *YouTube*, August 27, 2020. www.youtube.com.

FOR FURTHER RESEARCH

BOOKS

Phil Corso, *The Electoral College*. New York: PowerKids Press, 2020.

Tommy Jenkins, *Drawing the Vote: The Illustrated Guide to Voting in America*. New York: Abrams ComicArts, 2020.

Dr. Artika R. Tyner, *Black Voter Suppression: The Fight for the Right to Vote*. Minneapolis, MN: Lerner Publications, 2021.

INTERNET SOURCES

"Electoral College Fast Facts," *History, Art and Archives: United States House of Representatives*, n.d. https://history.house.gov.

"The Election Collection," *PBS Learning Media*, n.d. https://tpt.pbslearningmedia.org.

"Voting on Election Day," *USA.gov*, April 6, 2023. www.usa.gov.

WEBSITES

Ben's Guide to the US Government
https://bensguide.gpo.gov

Ben's Guide to the US Government provides activities, games, and fun facts about the government and the election process.

USA.gov
www.usa.gov

USA.gov provides information about the US government. It includes a section about voting, election laws, and election history.

Vote.gov
https://vote.gov

Vote.gov provides official information about voting requirements and voter registration.

INDEX

absentee voting, 20, 57
American Civil War, 38
American Woman Suffrage
Association (AWSA), 42–43
Anthony, Susan B., 42–43

ballot measures, 28
Biden, Joe, 51

candidates, 7, 9, 17, 19, 24–28, 31,
32, 34–35, 52
caucuses, 24–25, 27
congressional elections, 27–28

Dawes Act, 44–45
delegates, 25–27

election interference, 53–55
electoral college, 30–34
executive branch, 15

Federal Election Commission, 25
Fifteenth Amendment, 38, 44
first-past-the-post, 34
Fourteenth Amendment, 38

grandfather clauses, 40

instant-runoff voting, 35
Iroquois Nation, 44

judicial branch, 15

legislative branch, 15

mail-in ballots, 20, 46, 51–53
midterms, 28–29

National American Woman
Suffrage Association (NAWSA),
42–43
national party conventions, 25, 27
National Woman Suffrage
Association (NWSA), 42–43
National Woman's Party (NWP), 42
Nineteenth Amendment, 43

poll taxes, 39–41, 45
polling places, 6, 19–20, 49, 50
popular votes, 30–33
presidential elections, 6, 11, 24–27,
28, 30–31, 55, 57
primaries, 24, 26–27

Revolutionary War, 14

slavery, 37–38, 39
Snyder Act, 45

Thirteenth Amendment, 38
Trump, Donald, 33, 51, 55–56
two-round systems, 34–35

US Constitution, 15, 34, 37, 38, 41

voter fraud, 47, 50, 51, 56
voter suppression, 20–21, 47
voting machines, 9, 49, 55–56
Voting Rights Act, 40–41

IMAGE CREDITS

Cover: © LPETTET/iStockphoto
5: © LPETTET/iStockphoto
7: © The Toidi/Shutterstock Images
8: © Joseph Sohm/Shutterstock Images
10: © Joseph Sohm/Shutterstock Images
13: © andipantz/iStockphoto
16: © Rosamar/Shutterstock Images
18: © Trevor Bexon/Shutterstock Images
21: © Rob Crandall/Shutterstock Images
23: © michelmond/Shutterstock Images
26: © BestStockFoto/Shutterstock Images
29: © Matt Gush/Shutterstock Images
30: © Varga Jozsef Zoltan/Shutterstock Images
35: © Patti McConville/Alamy
37: © Keith Lance/iStockphoto
39: © Peter Pettus/Library of Congress
41: © George Grantham Bain Collection/Library of Congress
45: © Harris & Ewing Collection/Library of Congress
47: © Rob Crandall/Shutterstock Images
49: © Ringo Chiu/Shutterstock Images
50: © Richard Stephen/iStockphoto
54: © Joseph Sohm/Shutterstock Images
57: © Red Line Editorial

ABOUT THE AUTHOR

Sheryl Normandeau is the author of many nonfiction books for children and adults. Her work has been published internationally.